MY WORDS

ABOUT NATURE

BUGS

LILY
HOLLAND

DEBBIE
POWELL

OXFORD
UNIVERSITY PRESS

Note to Grown-ups

Learning lots of new words is a wonderful aid for young children's language development. A wide vocabulary also helps children to explore and understand the world around them as they grow and learn. Reading the words while looking at the pictures together creates a valuable learning experience.

This book includes new words as well as familiar ones. Even grown-ups might not know some of the words, and there is a pronunciation guide at the end of the book to help.

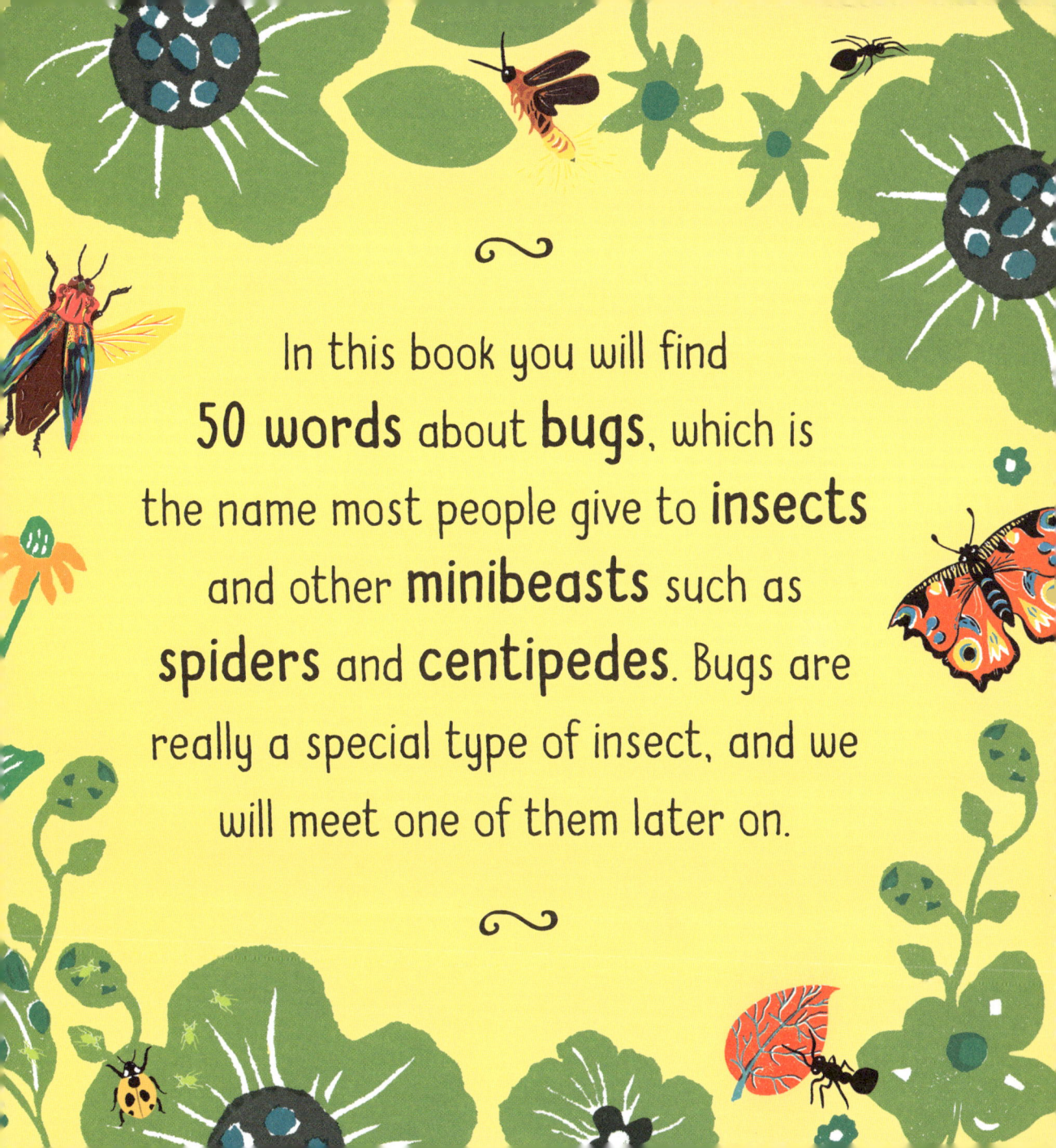

In this book you will find
50 words about **bugs**, which is
the name most people give to **insects**
and other **minibeasts** such as
spiders and **centipedes**. Bugs are
really a special type of insect, and we
will meet one of them later on.

This **bee** is an **insect**.

Insect bodies are in three parts:

a **head**

a **thorax**

an **abdomen**

And they all have
6 **legs**.

Buzzzzzz

A bee's **wings** move
so fast that they make
a buzzing sound.

Buzzzzz

Grasshoppers, **ants** and **dragonflies** are also insects.

An insect's skeleton is on the outside! It's called an **exoskeleton**.

Insects lay **eggs**.
These are ants' eggs.

Larvae
hatch out of
the eggs.

This insect is a **butterfly**.

Butterflies have beautiful wings.

They smell using their **antennae**.

They use a
long sucker called
a **proboscis**
to drink **nectar**
from flowers.

Caterpillars are larvae that hatch from butterfly eggs.

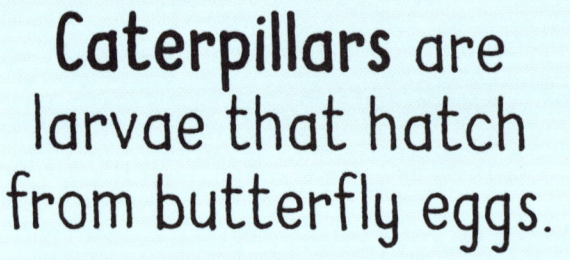

The caterpillar becomes a **chrysalis**.

This is called **metamorphosis**. Lots of other insects also go through metamorphosis.

After 10 days or so, a butterfly emerges from the chrysalis!

Spiders are **arachnids**, like **scorpions** and tiny **mites**.

All arachnids have eight legs.

This spider has spun a strong **web** from silk it makes inside its body.

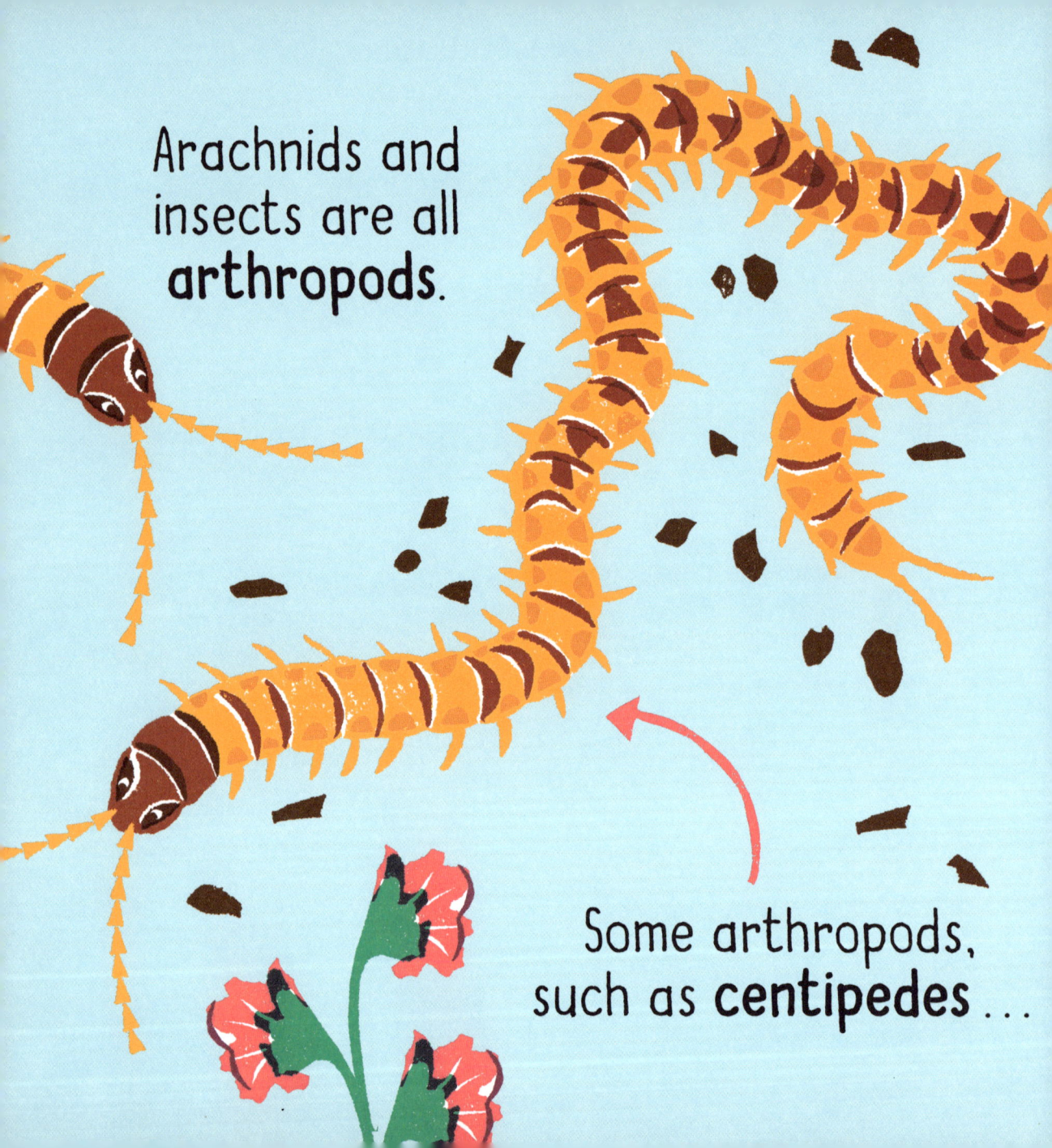

Arachnids and insects are all **arthropods**.

Some arthropods, such as **centipedes** . . .

...and **millipedes**, have lots of legs!

Beetles are insects that come in many sizes, shapes and colours.

Ladybirds are beetles that eat tiny insects called **aphids**.

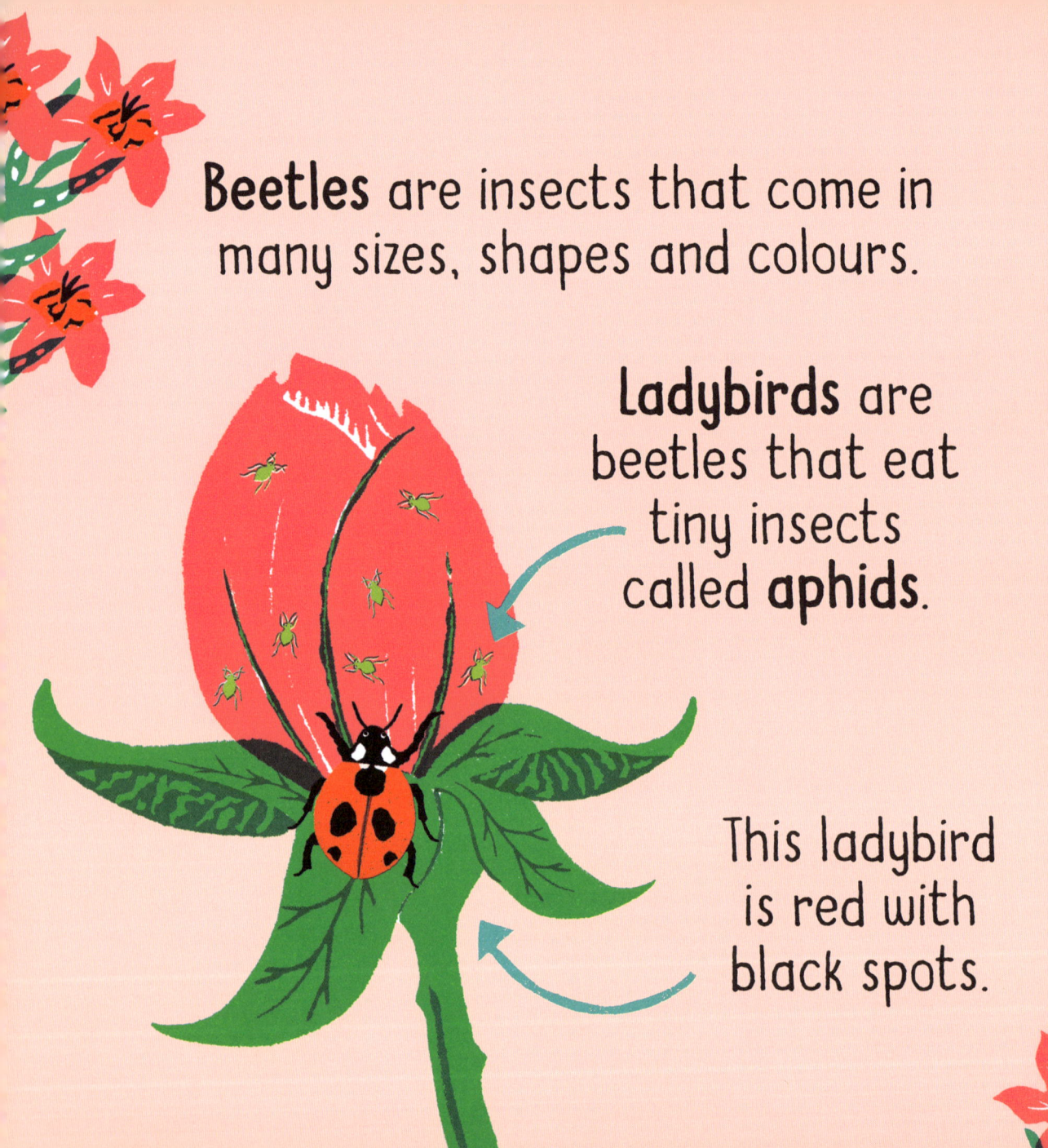

This ladybird is red with black spots.

This **stag beetle**'s **jaws** look like a deer's antlers.

Beetles have two pairs of wings.

The hard wings on the outside are called **elytra**.

Underneath them are the wings the beetle uses to fly.

The elytra are part of the beetle's **carapace**, which is tough like armour.

Some beetles have a colourful carapace.

These bugs
come out at night.
They are **nocturnal**.

Fireflies are
beetles that can
light themselves up
in the dark.

This is called
bioluminescence.

Scorpions have a sting
in their tail called
a **telson**. It is used
to kill their prey—the
small animals they eat.

Many **moths** are nocturnal, too.

Moths and butterflies are covered in tiny **scales**.

All moths have two **forewings** and two **hindwings**.

Some insects are **pollinators**, like these butterflies, bees and **hoverflies**.

When they land on flowers, tiny grains of powdery **pollen** stick to their legs and bodies.

Insects spread the pollen to other flowers, which helps the plants make seeds.

New plants grow from the seeds.

People who study insects are called **entomologists**.

Entomologists look very closely at insects and learn about how they live and behave.

Sometimes they identify new **species**, or types.

True bugs are insects with special **mouthparts** that pierce and suck.

This one is a **turquoise shield bug**.

fly

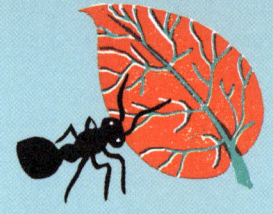

cricket

You could be like an entomologist and go on a bug hunt.

wasp

How many of the bugs in this book can you spot?

How many other words about bugs do you know?

hornet

earwig

termite